Andrew Lang

Twenty-Two and Ten

Thirty-Two Ballades in Blue China

Andrew Lang

Twenty-Two and Ten
Thirty-Two Ballades in Blue China

ISBN/EAN: 9783744776011

Printed in Europe, USA, Canada, Australia, Japan

Cover: Foto ©Thomas Meinert / pixelio.de

More available books at **www.hansebooks.com**

A BALLADE OF XXXII BALLADES.

Friend, when you bear a care-dulled eye,
And brow perplexed with things of weight,
And fain would bid some charm untie
The bonds that hold you all too strait,
Behold a solace to your fate,
Wrapped in this cover's china blue;
These ballades fresh and delicate,
This dainty troop of Thirty-two!

The mind, unwearied, longs to fly
And commune with the wise and great;
But that same ether, rare and high,
Which glorifies its worthy mate,
To breath forspent is disparate:
Laughing and light and airy-new
These come to tickle the dull pate,
This dainty troop of Thirty-two.

A BALLADE.

Most welcome then, when you and I,
Forestalling days for mirth too late,
To quips and cranks and fantasy
Some choice half-hour dedicate,
They weave their dance with measured rate
Of rhymes enlinked in order due,
Till frowns relax and cares abate,
This dainty troop of Thirty-two.

Envoy.

Princes, of toys that please your state
Quainter are surely none to view
Than these which pass with tripping gait,
This dainty troop of Thirty-two.

F. P.

XXXII BALLADES IN BLUE CHINA

XXXII BALLADES IN BLUE CHINA.

XXII and XXXII Ballades in Blue China

A. LANG

Tout *Soullas*

par

LONDON
KEGAN PAUL & CO., 1, PATERNOSTER SQUARE
MDCCCLXXXI

> "*Rondeaux*, BALLADES,
> *Chansons dizains, propos menus,*
> *Compte moy qu'ilz sont devenuz:*
> *Se faict il plus rien de nouveau?*"
>   CLEMENT MAROT, *Dialogue de deux*
>   *Amoureux.*

> "I love a ballad but even too well; if it be doleful matter, merrily set down, or a very pleasant thing indeed, and sung lamentably."
>   *A Winter's Tale*, Act iv. sc. 3.

TO

AUSTIN DOBSON.

CONTENTS.

	Page
Ballade of Theocritus	15
Ballade of Cleopatra's Needle	17
Ballade of Roulette	19
Ballade of Sleep	21
Ballade of the Midnight Forest	24
Ballade of the Tweed	27
Ballade of the Book-hunter	29
Ballade of the Voyage to Cythera	31
Ballade of the Summer Term	34
Ballade of the Muse	36
Ballade against the Jesuits	38
Ballade of Dead Cities	40
Ballade of the Royal Game of Golf	42
Double Ballade of Primitive Man	44
Ballade of Autumn	47
Ballade of True Wisdom	49
Ballade of Worldly Wealth	51

CONTENTS.

	Page
Ballade of Life	53
Ballade of Blue China	55
Ballade of Dead Ladies	57
Villon's Ballade of Good Counsel	59
Ballade of Rabbits and Hares	61
Valentine in form of Ballade	63
Ballade of Old Plays	65
Ballade of his Books	67
Ballade of Æsthetic Adjectives	69
Ballade of the Pleased Bard	72
Ballade for a Baby	74
Ballade Amoureuse	76
Ballade of Queen Anne	78
Ballade of Blind Love	80
Ballade of his Choice of a Sepulchre	82
Dizain	84

VERSES AND TRANSLATIONS.

A Portrait of 1783	87
The Moon's Minion	90
In Ithaca	92

CONTENTS.

xi

	Page
Homer	93
The Burial of Molière	94
Bion	95
Spring	96
Before the Snow	97
Villanelle	98
The Mystery of Queen Persephone	100
Stoker Bill	105
Natural Theology	108
The Odyssey	110
Ideal	111

BALLADE TO THEOCRITUS, IN WINTER.

ἰσορῶν τὰν Σικελὰν ἐς ἅλα.
                        Id. viii. 56.

Ah ! leave the smoke, the wealth, the roar
Of London, and the bustling street,
For still, by the Sicilian shore,
The murmur of the Muse is sweet.
Still, still, the suns of summer greet
The mountain-grave of Helikê,
And shepherds still their songs repeat
Where breaks the blue Sicilian sea.

What though they worship Pan no more,
That guarded once the shepherd's seat,
They chatter of their rustic lore,
They watch the wind among the wheat:

Cicalas chirp, the young lambs bleat,
Where whispers pine to cypress tree ;
They count the waves that idly beat
Where breaks the blue Sicilian sea.

Theocritus ! thou canst restore
The pleasant years, and over-fleet ;
With thee we live as men of yore,
We rest where running waters meet :
And then we turn unwilling feet
And seek the world—so must it be—
We may not linger in the heat
Where breaks the blue Sicilian sea !

ENVOY.

Master,—when rain, and snow, and sleet
And northern winds are wild, to thee
We come, we rest in thy retreat,
Where breaks the blue Sicilian sea !

BALLADE OF CLEOPATRA'S NEEDLE.

Ye giant shades of RA and TUM,
Ye ghosts of gods Egyptian,
If murmurs of our planet come
To exiles in the precincts wan
Where, fetish or Olympian,
To help or harm no more ye list,
Look down, if look ye may, and scan
This monument in London mist!

Behold, the hieroglyphs are dumb
That once were read of him that ran
When seistron, cymbal, trump, and drum
Wild music of the Bull began ;
When through the chanting priestly clan
Walk'd Ramses, and the high sun kiss'd
This stone, with blessing scored and ban—
This monument in London mist.

The stone endures though gods be numb;
Though human effort, plot, and plan
Be sifted, drifted, like the sum
Of sands in wastes Arabian.
What king may deem him more than man,
What priest says Faith can Time resist
While *this* endures to mark their span—
This monument in London mist?

ENVOY.

Prince, the stone's shade on your divan
Falls; it is longer than ye wist:
It preaches, as Time's gnomon can,
This monument in London mist!

BALLADE OF ROULETTE.

TO R. R.

This life—one was thinking to-day,
In the midst of a medley of fancies—
Is a game, and the board where we play
Green earth with her poppies and pansies.
Let *manque* be faded romances,
Be *passé* remorse and regret;
Hearts dance with the wheel as it dances—
The wheel of Dame Fortune's roulette.

The lover will stake as he may
His heart on his Peggies and Nancies;
The girl has her beauty to lay;
The saint has his prayers and his trances;
The poet bets endless expanses
In Dreamland; the scamp has his debt:
How they gaze at the wheel as it glances—
The wheel of Dame Fortune's roulette!

The Kaiser will stake his array
Of sabres, of Krupps, and of lances;
An Englishman punts with his pay,
And glory the *jeton* of France is;
Your artists, or Whistlers or Vances,
Have voices or colours to bet;
Will you moan that its motion askance is—
The wheel of Dame Fortune's roulette?

ENVOY.

The prize that the pleasure enhances?
The prize is—at last to forget
The changes, the chops, and the chances—
The wheel of Dame Fortune's roulette.

BALLADE OF SLEEP.

The hours are passing slow,
I hear their weary tread
Clang from the tower, and go
Back to their kinsfolk dead.
Sleep! death's twin brother dread!
Why dost thou scorn me so?
The wind's voice overhead
Long wakeful here I know,
And music from the steep
Where waters fall and flow.
Wilt thou not hear me, Sleep?

All sounds that might bestow
Rest on the fever'd bed,
All slumb'rous sounds and low
Are mingled here and wed,
And bring no drowsihed.

Shy dreams flit to and fro
With shadowy hair dispread;
With wistful eyes that glow,
And silent robes that sweep.
Thou wilt not hear me; no?
Wilt thou not hear me, Sleep?

What cause hast thou to show
Of sacrifice unsped?
Of all thy slaves below
I most have labourèd
With service sung and said;
Have cull'd such buds as blow,
Soft poppies white and red,
Where thy still gardens grow,
And Lethe's waters weep.
Why, then, art thou my foe?
Wilt thou not hear me, Sleep?

ENVOY.

Prince, ere the dark be shred
By golden shafts, ere low

And long the shadows creep:
Lord of the wand of lead,
Soft-footed as the snow,
Wilt thou not hear me, Sleep!

BALLADE OF THE MIDNIGHT FOREST.

AFTER THÉODORE DE BANVILLE.

Still sing the mocking fairies, as of old,
Beneath the shade of thorn and holly-tree;
The west wind breathes upon them, pure and
    cold,
And wolves still dread Diana roaming free
In secret woodland with her company.
'Tis thought the peasants' hovels know her
    rite
When now the wolds are bathed in silver
    light,
And first the moonrise breaks the dusky grey,
Then down the dells, with blown soft hair and
    bright,
And through the dim wood Dian threads her
    way.

With water-weeds twined in their locks of
    gold
The strange cold forest-fairies dance in glee,
Sylphs over-timorous and over-bold
Haunt the dark hollows where the dwarf may be,
The wild red dwarf, the nixies' enemy;
Then 'mid their mirth, and laughter, and
    affright,
The sudden Goddess enters, tall and white,
With one long sigh for summers pass'd away;
The swift feet tear the ivy nets outright
And through the dim wood Dian threads her way.

She gleans her silvan trophies; down the wold
She hears the sobbing of the stags that flee
Mixed with the music of the hunting roll'd,
But her delight is all in archery,
And naught of ruth and pity wotteth she
More than her hounds that follow on the flight;
The goddess draws a golden bow of might
And thick she rains the gentle shafts that slay.
She tosses loose her locks upon the night,
And through the dim wood Dian threads her way.

ENVOY.

Prince, let us leave the din, the dust, the spite,
The gloom and glare of towns, the plague, the blight :
Amid the forest leaves and fountain spray
There is the mystic home of our delight,
And through the dim wood Dian threads her way.

BALLADE OF THE TWEED.

(LOWLAND SCOTCH.)

TO T. W. LANG.

The ferox rins in rough Loch Awe,
A weary cry frae ony toun;
The Spey, that loups o'er linn and fa',
They praise a' ither streams aboon;
They boast their braes o' bonny Doon:
Gie *me* to hear the ringing reel,
Where shilfas sing, and cushats croon
By fair Tweed-side, at Ashiesteel!

There's Ettrick, Meggat, Ail, and a',
Where trout swim thick in May and June;
Ye'll see them take in showers o' snaw
Some blinking, cauldrife April noon:
Rax ower the palmer and march-broun,
And syne we'll show a bonny creel,
In spring or simmer, late or soon,
By fair Tweed-side, at Ashiesteel!

There's mony a water, great or sma',
Gaes singing in his siller tune,
Through glen and heugh, and hope and shaw,
Beneath the sun-licht or the moon :
But set us in our fishing-shoon
Between the Caddon-burn and Peel,
And syne we'll cross the heather broun
By fair Tweed-side at Ashiesteel !

ENVOY.

Deil take the dirty, trading loon
Wad gar the water ca' his wheel,
And drift his dyes and poisons doun
By fair Tweed-side at Ashiesteel !

BALLADE OF THE BOOK-HUNTER.

In torrid heats of late July,
In March, beneath the bitter *bise*,
He book-hunts while the loungers fly,—
He book-hunts, though December freeze;
In breeches baggy at the knees,
And heedless of the public jeers,
For these, for these, he hoards his fees,—
Aldines, Bodonis, Elzevirs.

No dismal stall escapes his eye,
He turns o'er tomes of low degrees,
There soiled romanticists may lie,
Or Restoration comedies;
Each tract that flutters in the breeze
For him is charged with hopes and fears,
In mouldy novels fancy sees
Aldines, Bodonis, Elzevirs.

With restless eyes that peer and spy,
Sad eyes that heed not skies nor trees,
In dismal nooks he loves to pry,
Whose motto evermore is *Spes!*
But ah! the fabled treasure flees;
Grown rarer with the fleeting years,
In rich men's shelves they take their ease,—
Aldines, Bodonis, Elzevirs!

ENVOY.

Prince, all the things that tease and please,—
Fame, hope, wealth, kisses, cheers, and tears,
What are they but such toys as these—
Aldines, Bodonis, Elzevirs?

BALLADE OF THE VOYAGE TO CYTHERA.

AFTER THÉODORE DE BANVILLE.

I know Cythera long is desolate ;
I know the winds have stripp'd the gardens
    green.
Alas, my friends ! beneath the fierce sun's
    weight
A barren reef lies where Love's flowers have
    been,
Nor ever lover on that coast is seen !
So be it, but we seek a fabled shore,
To lull our vague desires with mystic lore,
To wander where Love's labyrinths beguile ;
There let us land, there dream for evermore :
" It may be we shall touch the happy isle."

The sea may be our sepulchre. If Fate,
If tempests wreak their wrath on us, serene
We watch the bolt of heaven, and scorn the hate
Of angry gods that smite us in their spleen.
Perchance the jealous mists are but the screen
That veils the fairy coast we would explore.
Come, though the sea be vex'd, and breakers
    roar,
Come, for the air of this old world is vile,
Haste we, and toil, and faint not at the oar ;
"It may be we shall touch the happy isle."

Grey serpents trail in temples desecrate
Where Cypris smiled, the golden maid, the queen,
And ruined is the palace of our state ;
But happy Loves flit round the mast, and keen
The shrill wind sings the silken cords between.
Heroes are we, with wearied hearts and sore,
Whose flower is faded and whose locks are hoar,
Yet haste, light skiffs, where myrtle thickets
    smile ;
Love's panthers sleep 'mid roses, as of yore :
"It may be we shall touch the happy isle !"

ENVOY.

Sad eyes! the blue sea laughs, as heretofore.
Ah, singing birds your happy music pour!
Ah, poets, leave the sordid earth awhile;
Flit to these ancient gods we still adore:
" It may be we shall touch the happy isle!"

BALLADE OF THE SUMMER TERM.

(Being a Petition, in the form of a Ballade, praying the University Commissioners to spare the Summer Term.)

When Lent and Responsions are ended,
When May with fritillaries waits,
When the flower of the chestnut is splendid,
When drags are at all of the gates
(Those drags the philosopher "slates"
With a scorn that is truly sublime),*
Life wins from the grasp of the Fates
Sweet hours and the fleetest of time!

When wickets are bowl'd and defended,
When Isis is glad with "the Eights,"
When music and sunset are blended,
When Youth and the summer are mates,

* Cf. "Suggestions for Academic Reorganization."

When Freshmen are heedless of "Greats,"
And when note-books are cover'd with rhyme,
Ah, these are the hours that one rates—
Sweet hours and the fleetest of time!

When the brow of the Dean is unbended
At luncheons and mild tête-à-têtes,
When the Tutor's in love, nor offended
By blunders in tenses or dates;
When bouquets are purchased of Bates,
When the bells in their melody chime,
When unheeded the Lecturer prates—
Sweet hours and the fleetest of time!

ENVOY.

Reformers of Schools and of States,
Is mirth so tremendous a crime?
Ah! spare what grim pedantry hates—
Sweet hours and the fleetest of time!

BALLADE OF THE MUSE.

Quem tu, Melpomene, semel.

The man whom once, Melpomene,
Thou look'st on with benignant sight,
Shall never at the Isthmus be
A boxer eminent in fight,
Nor fares he foremost in the flight
Of Grecian cars to victory,
Nor goes with Delian laurels dight,
The man thou lov'st, Melpomene!

Not him the Capitol shall see,
As who hath crush'd the threats and might
Of monarchs, march triumphantly;
But Fame shall crown him, in his right
Of all the Roman lyre that smite
The first; so woods of Tivoli
Proclaim him, so her waters bright,
The man thou lov'st, Melpomene!

The sons of queenly Rome count *me*,
Me too, with them whose chants delight,—
The poets' kindly company;
Now broken is the tooth of spite,
But thou, that temperest aright
The golden lyre, all, all to thee
He owes—life, fame, and fortune's height—
The man thou lov'st, Melpomene !

ENVOY.

Queen, that to mute lips could'st unite
The wild swan's dying melody !
Thy gifts, ah ! how shall he requite—
The man thou lov'st, Melpomene?

BALLADE AGAINST THE JESUITS.

AFTER LA FONTAINE.

Rome does right well to censure all the vain
Talk of Jansenius, and of them who preach
That earthly joys are damnable! 'Tis plain
We need not charge at Heaven as at a breach;
No, amble on! We'll gain it, one and all;
The narrow path's a dream fantastical,
And Arnauld's quite superfluously driven
Mirth from the world   We'll scale the
    heavenly wall,
Escobar makes a primrose path to heaven!

He does not hold a man may well be slain
Who vexes with unseasonable speech,
You *may* do murder for five ducats gain,
Not for a pin, a ribbon, or a peach;
He ventures (most consistently) to teach

That there are certain cases that befall
When perjury need no good man appal,
And life of love (he says) may keep a leaven.
Sure, hearing this, a grateful world will bawl,
"Escobar makes a primrose path to heaven!"

" For God's sake read me somewhat in the strain
Of his most cheering volumes, I beseech!"
Why should I name them all? a mighty train—
So many, none may know the name of each.
Make these your compass to the heavenly beach,
These only in your library instal :
Burn Pascal and his fellows, great and small,
Dolts that in vain with Escobar have striven ;
I tell you, and the common voice doth call,
Escobar makes a primrose path to heaven !

ENVOY.

Satan, that pride did hurry to thy fall,
Thou porter of the grim infernal hall—
Thou keeper of the courts of souls unshriven !
To shun thy shafts, to 'scape thy hellish thrall,
Escobar makes a primrose path to heaven !

BALLADE OF DEAD CITIES.

TO E. W. GOSSE.

The dust of Carthage and the dust
Of Babel on the desert wold,
The loves of Corinth, and the lust,
Orchomenos increased with gold ;
The town of Jason, over-bold,
And Cherson, smitten in her prime—
What are they but a dream half-told?
Where are the cities of old time ?

In towns that were a kingdom's trust,
In dim Atlantic forests' fold,
The marble wasteth to a crust,
The granite crumbles into mould ;
O'er these—left nameless from of old—
As over Shinar's brick and slime,
One vast forgetfulness is roll'd—
Where are the cities of old time?

The lapse of ages, and the rust,
The fire, the frost, the waters cold,
Efface the evil and the just;
From Thebes, that Eriphyle sold,
To drown'd Caer-Is, whose sweet bells toll'd
Beneath the wave a dreamy chime
That echo'd from the mountain-hold, —
"Where are the cities of old time?"

ENVOY.

Prince, all thy towns and cities must
Decay as these, till all their crime,
And mirth, and wealth, and toil are thrust
Where are the cities of old time.

BALLADE OF THE ROYAL GAME OF GOLF.

(EAST FIFESHIRE.)

There are laddies will drive ye a ba'
To the burn frae the farthermost tee,
But ye mauna think driving is a',
Ye may heel her, and send her ajee,
Ye may land in the sand or the sea;
And ye're dune, sir, ye're no worth a preen,
Tak' the word that an auld man 'll gie,
Tak' aye tent to be up on the green!

The auld folk are crouse, and they craw
That their putting is pawky and slee;
In a bunker they're nae gude ava',
But to girn, and to gar the sand flee.
And a lassie can putt—ony she,—
Be she Maggy, or Bessie, or Jean,

But a cleek-shot's the billy for me,
Tak' aye tent to be up on the green!

I hae play'd in the frost and the thaw,
I hae play'd since the year thirty-three,
I hae play'd in the rain and the snaw,
And I trust I may play till I dee;
And I tell ye the truth and nae lee,
For I speak o' the thing I hae seen—
Tom Morris, I ken, will agree—
Tak' aye tent to be up on the green!

ENVOY.

Prince, faith you're improving a wee,
And, Lord, man, they tell me you're keen;
Tak' the best o' advice that can be,
Tak' aye tent to be up on the green!

DOUBLE BALLADE OF PRIMITIVE MAN.

TO J. A. FARRER.

He lived in a cave by the seas,
He lived upon oysters and foes,
But his list of forbidden degrees,
An extensive morality shows;
Geological evidence goes
To prove he had never a pan,
But he shaved with a shell when he chose,—
'Twas the manner of Primitive Man.

He worshipp'd the rain and the breeze,
He worshipp'd the river that flows,
And the Dawn, and the Moon, and the trees,
And bogies, and serpents, and crows;
He buried his dead with their toes
Tucked-up, an original plan,
Till their knees came right under their nose,—
'Twas the manner of Primitive Man.

His communal wives, at his ease,
He would curb with occasional blows :
Or his State had a queen, like the bees
(As another philosopher trows) :
When he spoke, it was never in prose,
But he sang in a strain that would scan,
For (to doubt it, perchance, were morose)
'Twas the manner of Primitive Man !

On the coasts that incessantly freeze,
With his stones, and his bones, and his bows ;
On luxuriant tropical leas,
Where the summer eternally glows,
He is found, and his habits disclose
(Let theology say what she can)
That he lived in the long, long agos,
'Twas the manner of Primitive Man !

From a status like that of the Crees,
Our society's fabric arose,—
Develop'd, evolved, if you please,
But deluded chronologists chose,

In a fancied accordance with Mos
es, 4000 B.C. for the span
When he rushed on the world and its woes,—
'Twas the manner of Primitive Man !

But the mild anthropologist,—*he's*
Not *recent* inclined to suppose
Flints Palæolithic like these,
Quaternary bones such as those !
In Rhinoceros, Mammoth and Co.'s,
First epoch, the Human began,
Theologians all to expose,—
'Tis the *mission* of Primitive Man.

ENVOY.

MAX, proudly your Aryans pose,
But their rigs they undoubtedly ran,
For, as every Darwinian knows,
'Twas the manner of Primitive Man !

BALLADE OF AUTUMN.

We built a castle in the air,
In summer weather, you and I,
The wind and sun were in your hair,—
Gold hair against a sapphire sky:
When Autumn came, with leaves that fly
Before the storm, across the plain,
You fled from me, with scarce a sigh—
My Love returns no more again!

The windy lights of Autumn flare:
I watch the moonlit sails go by;
I marvel how men toil and fare,
The weary business that they ply!
Their voyaging is vanity,
And fairy gold is all their gain,
And all the winds of winter cry,
"My Love returns no more again!"

Here, in my castle of Despair,
I sit alone with memory;
The wind-fed wolf has left his lair,
To keep the outcast company.
The brooding owl he hoots hard by,
The hare shall kindle on thy hearth-stane,
The Rhymer's soothest prophecy,—*
My Love returns no more again!

ENVOY.

Lady, my home until I die
Is here, where youth and hope were slain;
They flit, the ghosts of our July,
My Love returns no more again!

* Thomas of Ercildoune.

BALLADE OF TRUE WISDOM.

While others are asking for beauty or fame,
Or praying to know that for which they should
     pray,
Or courting Queen Venus, that affable dame,
Or chasing the Muses the weary and grey,
The sage has found out a more excellent way—
To Pan and to Pallas his incense he showers,
And his humble petition puts up day by day,
For a house full of books, and a garden of flowers.

Inventors may bow to the God that is lame,
And crave from the fire on his stithy a ray;
Philosophers kneel to the God without name,
Like the people of Athens, agnostics are they;
The hunter a fawn to Diana will slay,
The maiden wild roses will wreathe for the
     Hours;
But the wise man will ask, ere libation he pay,
For a house full of books, and a garden of flowers.

Oh ! grant me a life without pleasure or blame
(As mortals count pleasure who rush through
    their day
With a speed to which that of the tempest is
    tame) !
O grant me a house by the beach of a bay,
Where the waves can be surly in winter, and
    play
With the sea-weed in summer, ye bountiful
    powers !
And I'd leave all the hurry, the noise, and the
    fray,
For a house full of books, and a garden of
    flowers.

ENVOY.

Gods, grant or withhold it ; your "yea" and
    your "nay"
Are immutable, heedless of outcry of ours :
But life *is* worth living, and here we would stay
For a house full of books, and a garden of
    flowers.

BALLADE OF WORLDLY WEALTH.

(OLD FRENCH.)

Money taketh town and wall,
Fort and ramp without a blow ;
Money moves the merchants all,
While the tides shall ebb and flow ;
Money maketh Evil show
Like the Good, and Truth like lies :
These alone can ne'er bestow
Youth, and health, and Paradise.

Money maketh festival,
Wine she buys, and beds can strow ;
Round the necks of captains tall,
Money wins them chains to throw,
Marches soldiers to and fro,
Gaineth ladies with sweet eyes :
These alone can ne'er bestow
Youth, and health, and Paradise.

Money wins the priest his stall ;
Money mitres buys, I trow,
Red hats for the Cardinal,
Abbeys for the novice low ;
Money maketh sin as snow,
Place of penitence supplies :
These alone can ne'er bestow
Youth, and health, and Paradise.

BALLADE OF LIFE.

Dead and gone,'—a sorry burden of the Ballad of Life."
Death's Jest Book.

Say, fair maids, maying
In gardens green,
In deep dells straying,
What end hath been
Two Mays between
Of the flowers that shone
And your own sweet queen—
"They are dead and gone!"

Say, grave priests, praying
In dule and teen,
From cells decaying
What have ye seen
Of the proud and mean,
Of Judas and John,
Of the foul and clean?—
"They are dead and gone!"

Say, kings, arraying
Loud wars to win,
Of your manslaying
What gain ye glean?
"They are fierce and keen,
But they fall anon,
On the sword that lean,—
They are dead and gone!"

ENVOY.

Through the mad world's scene,
We are drifting on,
To this tune, I ween,
"They are dead and gone!"

BALLADE OF BLUE CHINA.

There's a joy without canker or cark,
There's a pleasure eternally new,
'Tis to gloat on the glaze and the mark
Of china that's ancient and blue;
Unchipp'd all the centuries through
It has pass'd, since the chime of it rang,
And they fashion'd it, figure and hue,
In the reign of the Emperor Hwang.

These dragons (their tails, you remark,
Into bunches of gillyflowers grew),—
When Noah came out of the ark,
Did these lie in wait for his crew?
They snorted, they snapp'd, and they slew
They were mighty of fin and of fang,
And their portraits Celestials drew
In the reign of the Emperor Hwang.

Here's a pot with a cot in a park,
In a park where the peach-blossoms blew,
Where the lovers eloped in the dark,
Lived, died, and were changed into two
Bright birds that eternally flew
Through the boughs of the may, as they sang ;
'Tis a tale was undoubtedly true
In the reign of the Emperor Hwang.

ENVOY.

Come, snarl at my ecstasies, do,
Kind critic, your "tongue has a tang"
But—a sage never heeded a shrew
In the reign of the Emperor Hwang.

BALLADE OF DEAD LADIES.

(AFTER VILLON.)

Nay, tell me now in what strange air
The Roman Flora dwells to-day,
Where Archippiada hides, and where
Beautiful Thais has passed away?
Whence answers Echo, afield, astray,
By mere or stream,—around, below?
Lovelier she than a woman of clay;
Nay, but where is the last year's snow?

Where is wise Héloïse, that care
Brought on Abeilard, and dismay?
All for her love he found a snare,
A maimed poor monk in orders grey;
And where's the Queen who willed to slay
Buridan, that in a sack must go
Afloat down Seine,—a perilous way—
Nay, but where is the last year's snow?

Where's that White Queen, a lily rare,
With her sweet song, the Siren's lay?
Where's Bertha Broad-foot, Beatrice fair?
Alys and Ermengarde, where are they?
Good Joan, whom English did betray
In Rouen town, and burned her? No,
Maiden and Queen, no man may say;
Nay, but where is the last year's snow?

ENVOY.

Prince, all this week thou need'st not pray,
Nor yet this year the thing to know.
One burden answers, ever and aye,
" Nay, but where is the last year's snow?"

VILLON'S BALLADE

OF GOOD COUNSEL, TO HIS FRIENDS OF EVIL LIFE.

Nay, be you pardoner or cheat,
Or cogger keen, or mumper shy,
You'll burn your fingers at the feat,
And howl like other folks that fry.
All evil folks that love a lie!
And where goes gain that greed amasses,
By wile, and trick, and thievery?
'Tis all to taverns and to lasses!

Rhyme, rail, dance, play the cymbals sweet,
With game, and shame, and jollity,
Go jigging through the field and street,
With *myst'ry* and *morality;*
Win gold at *gleek,*—and that will fly,
Where all you gain at *passage* passes,—
And that's? You know as well as I,
'Tis all to taverns and to lasses!

Nay, forth from all such filth retreat,
Go delve and ditch, in wet or dry,
Turn groom, give horse and mule their meat,
If you've no clerkly skill to ply ;
You'll gain enough, with husbandry,
But—sow hempseed and such wild grasses,
And where goes all you take thereby ?—
'Tis all to taverns and to lasses !

ENVOY.

Your clothes, your hose, your broidery,
Your linen that the snow surpasses,
Or ere they're worn, off, off they fly,
'Tis all to taverns and to lasses !

BALLADE OF RABBITS AND HARES.

In a vision a Sportsman forlorn
I beheld, in an isle of the West,
And his purple and linen were torn,
And he wailed, as he beat on his breast,—
" My people are men dispossessed,
They have vanished, and nobody cares,—
They have passed to the place of their rest,
They have gone with the Rabbits and Hares !

" Oh, why was a gentleman born
With a title, a name, and a crest,
Where the Rabbit is treated with scorn,
And the Hare is accounted a pest,
By the lumbering farmer repressed,
With his dogs, and his guns, and his snares ?
But my fathers have ended their quest,
They have gone with the Rabbits and Hares !

"Ah, woe for the clover and corn
That the Rabbit was wont to infest!
Ah, woe for my youth in its morn,
When the farmer obeyed my behest!
Happy days! like a wandering guest
Ye have fled, ye are sped unawares;
But my fathers are now with the blest,
They have gone with the Rabbits and Hares!

ENVOY.

Prince, mourn for a nation oppressed,
And absorbed in her stocks and her shares,
And bereaved of her bravest and best—
They have gone with the Rabbits and Hares!

VALENTINE IN FORM OF BALLADE.

The soft wind from the south land sped,
He set his strength to blow,
From forests where Adonis bled,
And lily flowers a-row:
He crossed the straits like streams that flow,
The ocean dark as wine,
To my true love to whisper low,
To be your Valentine.

The Spring half-raised her drowsy head,
Besprent with drifted snow,
"I'll send an April day," she said,
"To lands of wintry woe."
He came,—the winter's overthrow
With showers that sing and shine,
Pied daisies round your path to strow,
To be your Valentine.

Where sands of Egypt, swart and red,
'Neath suns Egyptian glow,
In places of the princely dead,
By the Nile's overflow,
The swallow preened her wings to go,
And for the North did pine,
And fain would brave the frost her foe,
To be your Valentine.

ENVOY.

Spring, Swallow, South Wind, even so,
Their various voice combine ;
But that they crave on *me* bestow,
To be your Valentine.

BALLADE OF OLD PLAYS.

(*Les Œuvres de Monsieur Molière. A Paris, chez Louys Billaine, à la Palme.* M.D.C.LXVI.)

LA COUR.

When these Old Plays were new, the King,
Beside the Cardinal's chair,
Applauded, 'mid the courtly ring,
The verses of Molière;
Point-lace was then the only wear,
Old Corneille came to woo,
And bright Du Parc was young and fair,
When these Old Plays were new!

LA COMÉDIE.

How shrill the butcher's cat-calls ring,
How loud the lackeys swear!
Black pipe-bowls on the stage they fling,
At Brécourt, fuming there!

The Porter's stabbed! a Mousquetaire
Breaks in with noisy crew—
'Twas all a commonplace affair
When these Old Plays were new!

LA VILLE.

When these Old Plays were new! They bring
A host of phantoms rare:
Old jests that float, old jibes that sting,
Old faces peaked with care:
Ménage's smirk, de Visé's stare,
The thefts of Jean Ribou,—*
Ah, publishers were hard to bear
When these Old Plays were new.

ENVOY.

Ghosts, at your Poet's word ye dare
To break Death's dungeons through,
And frisk, as in that golden air,
When these Old Plays were new!

* A knavish publisher.

BALLADE OF HIS BOOKS.

Here stand my books, line upon line
They reach the roof, and row by row,
They speak of faded tastes of mine,
And things I did, but do not, know:
Old school books, useless long ago,
Old Logics, where the spirit, railed in,
Could scarcely answer "yes" or "no"—
The many things I've tried and failed in!

Here's Villon, in morocco fine,
(The Poet starved, in mud and snow,)
Glatigny does not crave to dine,
And René's tears forget to flow.
And here's a work by Mrs. Crowe,
With hosts of ghosts and bogies jailed in;
Ah, all my ghosts have gone below—
The many things I've tried and failed in!

He's touched, this mouldy Greek divine,
The Princess D'Este's hand of snow;
And here the arms of D'Hoym shine,
And there's a tear-bestained Rousseau:
Here's Carlyle shrieking "woe on woe"
(The first edition, this, he wailed in);
I once believed in him—but oh,
The many things I've tried and failed in!

ENVOY.

Prince, tastes may differ; mine and thine
Quite other balances are scaled in;
May you succeed, though I repine—
"The many things I've tried and failed in!"

BALLADE OF ÆSTHETIC ADJECTIVES.

There be "subtle" and "sweet," that are bad ones to beat,
There are " lives unlovely," and " souls astray ;"
There is much to be done yet with "moody" and "meet,"
And "ghastly," and "grimly," and "gaunt," and "grey ;"
We should ever be "blithesome," but never be gay,
And "splendid" is suited to "summer" and "sea ;"
"Consummate," they say, is enjoying its day,—
" Intense" is the adjective dearest to me !

The Snows and the Rose they are "windy" and
    "fleet,"
And "frantic" and "faint" are Delight and
    Dismay;
Yea, "sanguine," it seems, as the juice of the
    beet,
Are "the hands of the King" in a general way:
There be loves that quicken, and sicken, and
    slay;
"Supreme" is the song of the Bard of the
    free;
But of adjectives all that I name in my lay,
"Intense" is the adjective dearest to me!

The Matron intense—let us sit at her feet,
And pelt her with lilies as long as we may;
The Maiden intense—is not always discreet;
But the Singer intense, in his "singing array,"
Will win all the world with his roundelay:
While "blithe" birds carol from tree to
    tree,
And Art unto Nature doth simper, and say,—
"'Intense' is the adjective dearest to me!"

ENVOY.

Prince, it is surely as good as a play
To mark how the poets and painters agree ;
But of plumage æsthetic that feathers the jay,
" Intense" is the adjective dearest to me!

BALLADE OF THE PLEASED BARD.

They call me "dull," "affected," "tame;"
My Muse "has neither voice nor wing;"
My prose (though lucrative) is "lame,"
My satires, "wasps without the sting."
The Critic thus—Opprobrious thing!—
No more I heed or hear his chaff,
Nor note the ink that he may sling—
A Lady wants my autograph!

All heedless of the common blame,
My muse her random rhymes will string;
The Boers may shoot, the Irish "schame,"
The world and all its woes go swing!
My heart has ceased from sorrowing,
I grasp Apollo's laurell'd staff,
And cry aloud, like anything,—
A Lady wants my autograph!

Oh Flatt'ry, soft, delicious flame !
Oh, fairer than the flowers of Spring,
These blossoms of the noblest name
A lady's good enough to fling !
Ah, tie them with a silver string,
Crown, crown the bowl with shandygaff,
And shout, till all the welkin ring,—
"A Lady wants my autograph !"

ENVOY.

Princess, my lips can never frame
My whole acknowledgments, or half;
For this, I feel, at last, is fame—
A Lady wants my autograph !

BALLADE FOR A BABY.

(FROM "THE GARLAND OF RACHEL.")

'Tis distance lends, the poet says,
Enchantment to the view,
And this makes possible the praise
Which I bestow on you.
For babies rosy-pink of hue
I do not *always* care,
But distance paints the mountains blue,
And Rachel always fair.

Ah Time, speed on her flying days,
Bring back my youth that flew,
That she may listen to my lays
Where Merton stock-doves coo;
That I may sing afresh, anew,
My songs, now faint and rare,
Time, make me always twenty-two,
And Rachel always fair.

Nay, long ago, down dusky ways
Fled Cupid and his crew;
Life brings not back the morning haze,
The dawning and the dew;
And other lips must sigh and sue,
And younger lovers dare
To hint that Love is always true,
And Rachel always fair.

ENVOY.

Princess, let Age bid Youth adieu,
Adieu to this despair,
To me, who thus despairing woo,
And Rachel always fair.

BALLADE AMOUREUSE.

AFTER FROISSART.

Not Jason nor Medea wise,
I crave to see, nor win much lore,
Nor list to Orpheus' minstrelsies;
Nor Her'cles would I see, that o'er
The wide world roamed from shore to shore;
Nor, by St. James, Penelope,—
Nor pure Lucrece, such wrong that bore:
To see my Love suffices me!

Virgil and Cato, no man vies
  With them in wealth of clerkly store;
I would not see them with mine eyes;
Nor him that sailed, *sans* sail nor oar,
Across the barren sea and hoar,
And all for love of his ladye;
Nor pearl nor sapphire takes me more:
To see my Love suffices me!

I heed not Pegasus, that flies
As swift as shafts the bowmen pour;
Nor famed Pygmalion's artifice,
Whereof the like was ne'er before;
Nor Oleus, that drank of yore
The salt wave of the whole great sea :
Why? dost thou ask? 'Tis as I swore—
To see my Love suffices me!

BALLADE OF QUEEN ANNE.

The modish Airs,
The Tansey Brew,
The *Swains* and *Fairs*
In curtained Pew;
Nymphs KNELLER drew,
Books BENTLEY read,—
Who knows them, who?
QUEEN ANNE is dead!

We buy her Chairs,
Her China blue,
Her red-brick Squares
We build anew;
But ah! we rue,
When all is said,
The tale o'er-true,
QUEEN ANNE is dead!

Now *Bulls* and *Bears*,
A ruffling Crew,
With Stocks and Shares,
With Turk and Jew,
Go bubbling through
The Town ill-bred :
The World's askew,
QUEEN ANNE is dead !

ENVOY.

Friend, praise the new ;
The old is fled :
Vivat FROU-FROU !
QUEEN ANNE is dead !

BALLADE OF BLIND LOVE.

(AFTER LYONNET DE COISMES.)

Who have loved and ceased to love, forget
That ever they loved in their lives, they say;
Only remember the fever and fret,
And the pain of Love, that was all his pay;
All the delight of him passes away
From hearts that hoped; and from lips that
    met—
Too late did I love you, my love, and yet
I shall never forget till my dying day.

Too late were we 'ware of the secret net
That meshes the feet in the flowers that stray;
There were we taken and snared, Lisette,
In the dungeon of 𝔏𝔞 𝔉𝔞𝔲𝔰𝔰𝔢 𝔄𝔪𝔦𝔰𝔱𝔦𝔢;
Help was there none in the wide world's fray,
Joy was there none in the gift and the debt;

Too late we knew it, too long regret —
I shall never forget till my dying day!

We must live our lives, though the sun be set,
Must meet in the masque where parts we play,
Must cross in the maze of Life's minuet;
Our yea is yea, and our nay is nay:
But while snows of winter or flowers of May
Are the sad year's shroud or coronet,
In the season of rose or of violet,
I shall never forget till my dying day!

ENVOY.

Queen, when the clay is my coverlet,
When I am dead, and when you are grey,
Vow, where the grass of the grave is wet,
" I shall never forget till my dying day!"

BALLADE OF HIS CHOICE OF A SEPULCHRE.

Here I'd come when weariest !
    Here the breast
Of the Windburg's tufted over
Deep with bracken ; here his crest
    Takes the west,
Where the wide-winged hawk doth hover.

Silent here are lark and plover ;
    In the cover
Deep below the cushat best
Loves his mate, and croons above her
    O'er their nest,
Where the wide-winged hawk doth hover

Bring me here, Life's tired-out guest,
    To the blest
Bed that waits the weary rover,

Here should failure be confessed ;
    Ends my quest,
Where the wide-winged hawk doth hover!

ENVOY.

Friend, or stranger kind, or lover,
Ah, fulfil a last behest,
    Let me rest
Where the wide-winged hawk doth hover!

DIZAIN.

As, to the pipe, with rhythmic feet
In windings of some old-world dance,
The smiling couples cross and meet,
Join hands, and then in line advance,
So, to these fair old tunes of France,
Through all their maze of to-and-fro,
The light-heeled numbers laughing go,
Retreat, return, and ere they flee,
One moment pause in panting row,
And seem to say—Vos plaudite!

A. D.

VERSES AND TRANSLATIONS.

ORONTE.—*Ce ne sont point de ces grands vers pompeux,
Mais de petits vers!*
"Le Misanthrope," Acte i., Sc. 2.

A PORTRAIT OF 1783.

Your hair and chin are like the hair
And chin Burne-Jones's ladies wear;
You were unfashionably fair
    In '83;
And sad you were when girls are gay,
You read a book about *Le vrai
Mérite de l'homme*, alone in May.
    What *can* it be,
Le vrai mérite de l'homme? Not gold,
Not titles that are bought and sold,
Not wit that flashes and is cold,
    But Virtue merely!
Instructed by Jean-Jacques Rousseau
(And Jean-Jacques, surely, ought to know),
You bade the crowd of foplings go,
    You glanced severely,

Dreaming beneath the spreading shade
Of 'that vast hat the Graces made;'*
So Rouget sang—while yet he played
    With courtly rhyme,
And hymned great Doisi's red perruque,
And Nice's eyes, and Zulmé's look,
And dead canaries, ere he shook
    The sultry time
With strains like thunder. Loud and low
Methinks I hear the murmur grow,
The tramp of men that come and go
    With fire and sword.
They war against the quick and dead,
Their flying feet are dashed with red,
As theirs the vintaging that tread
    Before the Lord.

   * Vous y verrez, belle Julie,
    Que ce chapeau tout maltraité
    Fut, dans un instant de folie,
    Par les Grâces même inventé.
'À Julie.' *Essais en Prose et en Vers*, par Joseph Lisle; Paris. An. V. de la République.

O head unfashionably fair,
What end was thine, for all thy care?
We only see thee dreaming there :
    We cannot see
The breaking of thy vision, when
The Rights of Man were lords of men,
When virtue won her own again
    In '93.

THE MOON'S MINION.

(FROM THE PROSE OF C. BAUDELAIRE.)

Thine eyes are like the sea, my dear,
  The wand'ring waters, green and grey;
Thine eyes are wonderful and clear,
  And deep, and deadly, even as they;
The spirit of the changeful sea
  Informs thine eyes at night and noon,
She sways the tides, and the heart of thee,
  The mystic, sad, capricious Moon!

The Moon came down the shining stair,
  Of clouds that fleck the summer sky,
She kissed thee, saying, "Child, be fair,
  And madden men's hearts, even as I;
Thou shalt love all things strange and sweet,
  That know me and are known of me;
The lover thou shalt never meet,
  The land where thou shalt never be!"

She held thee in her chill embrace,
    She kissed thee with cold lips divine,
She left her pallor on thy face,
    That mystic ivory face of thine;
And now I sit beside thy feet,
    And all my heart is far from thee,
Dreaming of her I shall not meet,
    And of the land I shall not see!

IN ITHACA.

"And now am I greatly repenting that ever I left my life with thee, and the immortality thou didst promise me."—*Letter of Odysseus to Calypso.* Luciani *Vera Historia.*

'Tis thought Odysseus when the strife was o'er
  With all the waves and wars, a weary while,
  Grew restless in his disenchanted isle,
And still would watch the sunset, from the shore,
Go down the ways of gold, and evermore
  His sad heart followed after, mile on mile,
  Back to the Goddess of the magic wile,
Calypso, and the love that was of yore.

Thou too, thy haven gained, must turn thee yet
  To look across the sad and stormy space,
  Years of a youth as bitter as the sea,
Ah, with a heavy heart, and eyelids wet,
  Because, within a fair forsaken place
  The life that might have been is lost to thee.

HOMER.

Homer, thy song men liken to the sea
    With all the notes of music in its tone,
    With tides that wash the dim dominion
Of Hades, and light waves that laugh in glee
Around the isles enchanted ; nay, to me
    Thy verse seems as the River of source
        unknown
    That glasses Egypt's temples overthrown
In his sky-nurtured stream, eternally.

No wiser we than men of heretofore
    To find thy sacred fountains guarded fast ;
Enough, thy flood makes green our human
        shore,
    As Nilus Egypt, rolling down his vast
His fertile flood, that murmurs evermore
    Of gods dethroned, and empires in the past.

THE BURIAL OF MOLIÈRE.

(AFTER J. TRUFFIER.)

Dead—he is dead! The rouge has left a trace
  On that thin cheek where shone, perchance,
    a tear,
  Even while the people laughed that held
    him dear
But yesterday. He died,—and not in grace,
And many a black-robed caitiff starts apace
  To slander him whose *Tartuffe* made them
    fear,
And gold must win a passage for his bier,
And bribe the crowd that guards his resting-
    place.

Ah, Molière, for that last time of all,
  Man's hatred broke upon thee, and went by,
And did but make more fair thy funeral.
  Though in the dark they hid thee stealthily,
Thy coffin had the cope of night for pall,
  For torch, the stars along the windy sky!

BION.

The wail of Moschus on the mountains crying
    The Muses heard, and loved it long ago;
They heard the hollows of the hills replying,
    They heard the weeping water's overflow;
They winged the sacred strain—the song undying,
    The song that all about the world must go,—
When poets for a poet dead are sighing,
    The minstrels for a minstrel friend laid low.

And dirge to dirge that answers, and the weeping
    For Adonais by the summer sea,
The plaints for Lycidas, and Thyrsis (sleeping
    Far from 'the forest ground called Thessaly'),
These hold thy memory, Bion, in their keeping,
    And are but echoes of the moan for thee.

SPRING.

(AFTER MELEAGER.)

Now the bright crocus flames, and now
    The slim narcissus takes the rain,
And, straying o'er the mountain's brow,
    The daffodilies bud again.
    The thousand blossoms wax and wane
On wold, and heath, and fragrant bough,
But fairer than the flowers art thou,
    Than any growth of hill or plain.

Ye gardens, cast your leafy crown,
That my Love's feet may tread it down,
    Like lilies on the lilies set;
My Love, whose lips are softer far
Than drowsy poppy petals are,
    And sweeter than the violet!

BEFORE THE SNOW.

(AFTER ALBERT GLATIGNY.)

The winter is upon us, not the snow,
   The hills are etched on the horizon bare,
   The skies are iron grey, a bitter air,
The meagre cloudlets shudder to and fro.
One yellow leaf the listless wind doth blow,
   Like some strange butterfly, unclassed and
      rare.
Your footsteps ring in frozen alleys, where
The black trees seem to shiver as you go.

Beyond lie church and steeple, with their old
   And rusty vanes that rattle as they veer,
A sharper gust would shake them from their
      hold,
   Yet up that path, in summer of the year,
And past that melancholy pile we strolled
   To pluck wild strawberries, with merry cheer.

VILLANELLE.

TO LUCIA.

Apollo left the golden Muse
   And shepherded a mortal's sheep,
Theocritus of Syracuse!

To mock the giant swain that woo's
   The sea-nymph in the sunny deep,
Apollo left the golden Muse.

Afield he drove his lambs and ewes,
   Where Milon and where Battus reap,
Theocritus of Syracuse!

To watch thy tunny-fishers cruise
   Below the dim Sicilian steep
Apollo left the golden Muse.

Ye twain did loiter in the dews,
   Ye slept the swain's unfever'd sleep,
Theocritus of Syracuse!

That Time might half with *his* confuse
Thy songs,—like his, that laugh and leap,—
Theocritus of Syracuse,
Apollo left the golden Muse!

THE MYSTERY OF QUEEN PERSEPHONE.

St. Paul and the Devil disputing about the Immortality of Man's Soul, and St. Paul maintaining the same, (from the similitude of the corn-seed sown, which again sprouteth,) the Devil refutes him by his atheistic subtlety, but is put to shame by the evidence of three witnesses, namely, Persephone, Hela, and St. Lucy.

The Scene is Mount Gerizim.

Intrabunt Sanctus Paulus, et Diabolus, inter se de immortalitate Animae disputantes.

SANCTUS PAULUS.

Ye say that when a man is dead
He never more shall lift his head,
As doth the flower perishèd,
Nor break ne sweet ne bitter bread.
   I hold you much in scorn !
Lo, if you cast in earth a seed
That seemeth to be dead indeed,
   I wot ye shall have corn ;

And all men shall rejoice and reap :
And so it fares with them that sleep,
The narrow house doth them but keep
    Until the judgment morn.

DIABOLUS.

There is an end of grief and mirth,
    There is an end of all things born,
And if ye sow into the earth
    A seed, ye shall have corn ;
    But if ye sow its withered root
    It shall not bear you any fruit,
    It will not sprout and spring again ;
    And if ye look to gather grain,
    Of men mote ye have scorn.
Man's body buried is the sown
Dead root, whose flower is over-blown.

SANCTUS PAULUS.

Beshrew thee for thy subtleties
That melt the hearts of men with lies,
An evil task hath he that tries
    To still thy subtle tongue !

But look ye round and ye shall see
The Dames that Queens of dead men be,
I wot there are no mo than three,
    When all is said and sung.

Hic intrabunt et cantabunt tres Reginæ.

PERSEPHONE.

I am the Queen Persephone.
The lips of Grecians prayed to me,
    Saying, I give men sleep;
But I would have ye well to know
That with me none do slumber so;
    But there be some that weep,
And juster souls content to dwell
Among the fields of asphodel,
    By the Nine Waters deep.

HELA.

I am the Queen of Hela's House,
Great clouds I bind upon my brows;
    Night for a covering.
For them I hold, I will ye wot

They sorrow, but they slumber not,
    They have no lust to sing,
And never comes a merry voice,
Nor doth a soul of them rejoice
    Until their uprising.

SANCTA LUCIA.

I am a Queen of Paradise,
And who shall look on me, I wis,
    His spirit shall find grace.
Whoso dwells with me walks along
In gardens glad with small birds' song,
    A flowered and grassy place,
Therein the souls of blessèd men
Wait each, till comes his love again,
    To look upon her face!

SANCTUS PAULUS.

Thou, Sir Diabolus, art shent,
I wot that well ye might repent,
But till Midsummer fall in Lent,
    Ye will not cease to sin.

Get thee to dungeon underground
And sit beside thy man, Mahound.
I wot I would ye twain were bound
For evermore therein.

Fugiat Diabolus ad locum suum.

STOKER BILL.

A BALLAD OF THE SCHOOL-BOARD FLEET.

    Which my name is Stoker Bill,
    And a pleasant berth I fill,
And the care the ladies take of me is clipping;
    They have made me pretty snug,
    With a blooming Persian rug,
In the Ladies' new Æsthetic Training
    Shipping.

    There's my Whistler pastels, there,
    As are quite beyond compare,
And a portrait of Miss Connie Gilchrist skipping;
    From such art we all expect
    Quite a softening effect,
In the Ladies' new Æsthetic Training
    Shipping.

And my beer comes in a mug—
Such a rare old Rhodian jug!
And here I sits æsthetically sipping;
And I drinks my grog or ale
On a chair by Chippendale—
We've no others in our modern training
    shipping.

There's our first Liftenant, too,
Is a rare old (China) Blue,
And you do not very often catch him tripping
At a monogram or mark,
But no more than Noah's ark,
Does he know the way to manage this here
    shipping.

But the Boys? the Boys, they stands
With white lilies in their hands,
And they do not know the meaning of a whip-
    ping:
For the whole delightful ship is
Like a dream of Lippo Lippi's,
More than what you mostly see in modern
    shipping.

Well, some coves they cuts up rough,
And they calls æsthetics stuff,
And they says as we've no business to keep
 dipping
In the rates, but ladies likes it,
And our flag we never strikes it—
Bless old England's new Æsthetic Training
 Shipping!

NATURAL THEOLOGY.

ἐπεὶ καὶ τοῦτον ὄιομαι ἀθανάτοισιν
εὔχεσθαι· Πάντες δὲ θεῶν χατέουσ' ἄνθρωποι.
OD. III. 47.

"Once CAGN was like a father, kind and good,
But He was spoiled by fighting many things;
He wars upon the lions in the wood,
   And breaks the Thunder-bird's tremendous
         wings;
But still we cry to Him,— *We are thy brood*—
O Cagn, be merciful! and us He brings
To herds of elands, and great store of food,
   And in the desert opens water-springs."

So Qing, King Nqsha's Bushman hunter, spoke,
   Beside the camp-fire, by the fountain fair,

When all were weary, and soft clouds of smoke
Were fading, fragrant, in the twilit air :
And suddenly in each man's heart there woke
A pang, a sacred memory of prayer.

THE ODYSSEY.

As one that for a weary space has lain
    Lulled by the song of Circe and her wine
    In gardens near the pale of Proserpine,
Where that Ææan isle forgets the main,
And only the low lutes of love complain,
    And only shadows of wan lovers pine,
    As such an one were glad to know the brine
Salt on his lips, and the large air again,—
So gladly, from the songs of modern speech
    Men turn, and see the stars, and feel the free
        Shrill wind beyond the close of heavy
            flowers,
        And through the music of the languid
            hours,
They hear like ocean on a western beach
    The surge and thunder of the Odyssey.

IDEAL.

Suggested by a female head in wax, of unknown date, but supposed to be either of the best Greek age, or a work of Raphael or Leonardo. It is now in the Lille Museum.

Ah, mystic child of Beauty, nameless maid,
   Dateless and fatherless, how long ago,
A Greek, with some rare sadness overweighed,
   Shaped thee, perchance, and quite forgot his woe!
Or Raphael thy sweetness did bestow,
While magical his fingers o'er thee strayed,
   Or that great pupil of Verrocchio
Redeemed thy still perfection from the shade

That hides all fair things lost, and things unborn,
   Where one has fled from me, that wore thy grace,

And that grave tenderness of thine awhile ;
Nay, still in dreams I see her, but her face
Is pale, is wasted with a touch of scorn,
And only on thy lips I find her smile.

THE END.

CHISWICK PRESS :—CHARLES WHITTINGHAM AND CO.
TOOKS COURT, CHANCERY LANE.

www.ingramcontent.com/pod-product-compliance
Lightning Source LLC
Chambersburg PA
CBHW020140170426
43199CB00010B/823